KILLER BEES

REVISED EDITION

LAURENCE PRINGLE

Morrow Junior Books   New York

The author wishes to thank Dr. Orley R. Taylor, Department of Entomology—Snow Entomological Museum, University of Kansas, for reading the manuscript of this book and helping to improve its accuracy.

PHOTO CREDITS: Permission for the following photographs is gratefully acknowledged: Beekeeping Education Service, Cheshire, CT, pp. 3 (© 1978 Ray Williamson, from "Life History and Activities of the Honeybee "), 4, 38 (© 1984 Ray Williamson, from "The Amazing World of the Honeybee"), 7 (right) (© 1984 Dewey M. Caron, from "The Africanized Honeybee in the Americas"); California Department of Food and Agriculture, pp. viii, 20, 43 (both); Anita Collins, p. 35; Troy Fore, Jr., *The Speedy Bee,* p. 15; Oak Ridge National Laboratory, p. 23; Laurence Pringle, pp. 7 (left), 10; David Roubik, p. 36; William Rubink, p. 30; University of Kansas, Office of University Relations, p. 24; Visuals Unlimited, p. 13 (photo David Phillips).

HC 1 2 3 4 5 6 7 8 9 10
PA 1 2 3 4 5 6 7 8 9 10

Library of Congress Cataloging-in-Publication Data

Pringle, Laurence P.
Killer bees / Laurence Pringle.—
Rev. ed.
p.   cm.
Rev. ed. of: Here come the killer bees. c1986.

Summary: Describes the characteristics and behavior of Africanized bees and discusses how they came to Brazil, how they have now spread northward as far as the United States, and their potentially disruptive influence on the native honeybee population, crop yields, and the honey and beeswax industry.

ISBN 0-688-09617-4.   ISBN 0-688-09524-0 (lib. bdg.).   ISBN 0-688-09618-2 (pbk.)

1. Africanized honeybee—Juvenile literature. [1. Africanized honeybee. 2. Bees.] I. Pringle, Laurence P. Here come the killer bees. II Title.
QL568.A6P76   1990
595.79'9—dc20   90-34658   CIP   AC

CONTENTS

"The Africanized bee problem is real. It is rich with biological, economic, social, and political complications. It will be with us for a long time."

Dr. Orley Taylor
Department of Entomology
University of Kansas

from *Science* magazine,
October 17, 1980

INTRODUCTION

We will never know exactly when and where the first swarm of killer bees flew into the United States. They crossed from Mexico into Texas, near Brownsville, in fall 1990.

By the time a colony of these bees had been found and identified, other swarms had probably also established nests. Flights across the border from Mexico continued and increased. The long-awaited killer bee invasion of the United States was under way.

Descendants of bees from Africa, these honeybees spread outward from Brazil after their release there in 1957. Their fame also spread as newspapers and other media described hundreds of these bees stinging and sometimes killing people. Television viewers saw *The Swarm* and other sensational films about the bees. No wonder the term *killer bees* caught on with the public.

Entomologists, scientists who study insects, prefer to call them *Africanized* or, simply, *African bees.* For reasons explained in Chapter 4, they are called African bees in this book. Entomologists say that the threat of death and injury from these bees has been greatly exaggerated.

They are deeply concerned, however, that African bees will disrupt the entire honey and beeswax industry in the United States. Even worse, the bees may cause a reduction in the yield of many agricultural crops that are now pollinated by other varieties of honeybees.

The first edition of this book, published in 1986, traced the spread of African bees through Central America. Now the bees have reached the United States. It is vital for people to know more about the behavior of African bees and the difficulties they may cause.

The first two chapters, changed little from the earlier edition, tell why African bees behave as they do, and about their impact in South and Central America. The rest of the book emphasizes events and discoveries since 1986, and the challenges we may face from African bees in the United States.

KILLER BEES

A young killer bee, with its tongue sticking out, hatches from its cell. These highly defensive honeybees have now invaded the United States.

1

CLIMATE SHAPED THEIR LIVES

"Honey maker" is the meaning of the Latin word *Apis,* the genus of insects we call honeybees. Around the world, all species and subspecies of *Apis* are alike in many ways. All honeybees are social insects that live in colonies of up to sixty thousand bees. Each colony has a single *queen.* She may live several years, and she lays all the eggs from which *drones* (males) and *workers* (infertile females) develop. Worker bees secrete wax and with it build thousands of hexagonal cells. In some cells, eggs are deposited and develop into young bees; in others, honey is stored.

Worker bees are also the honey makers. They sip nectar from flowers and in the process spread pollen from one blossom to another. This accidental pollination service is vital to the successful reproduction of many plants. Within the crop of a worker bee, nectar is partially digested into simple sugars and then regurgitated as honey into the cells of the bee's nest.

When a honeybee colony grows too large for its nest space, a process called *swarming* often occurs. Worker bees lead their colony's queen to a new nest site; she is accompanied by about half of the colony's drones and workers. A new queen soon hatches and stays with the bees that remain.

There is still doubt about whether honeybees originated in Asia or Africa, but entomologists agree that the original honeybees evolved into several species and subspecies as they spread through the Old World, adapting to new environments. Climate had a powerful effect on the evolution of honeybees.

To survive in Europe, bees adapted to a temperate climate—warm in summer, cold in winter. Nests inside well-insulated hollows help honeybees survive the winter. Within their shelters and near their stored honey, they form a *winter cluster*—a large, continually moving sphere. Because this activity requires energy, honeybees of temperate regions store lots of honey, some of which they consume in winter.

Climate also influenced the swarming behavior of honeybees that evolved in Europe. Honeybees that live in temperate regions usually swarm early and just once

*A queen honeybee lowers her abdomen into a honeycomb cell and lays an egg.
By early summer, she may lay as many as 2,000 eggs a day. She may produce
a half million eggs in her lifetime.*

Worker honeybees do almost all their colony's work—building, cleaning, food foraging, and defense.

in the flowering season. This allows the colony time to store enough honey for its vital winter rations.

All worker honeybees have the ability to sting in order to defend the colony's young and stored food. However, the varieties of bees that evolved in temperate regions often did not have to defend their nests. Snug in hollow trees or other protected cavities, they had few enemies. They stung bears that tried to steal their honey, but they were not nearly as quick to sting as, for example, the kind of wasps called yellow jackets, which live in less secure nests.

After domesticating honeybees in Europe, people began to crossbreed different varieties, trying to get the best characteristics for their purposes. They wanted bees that were good honey producers, resistant to disease, and easy to handle. Today the gentlest types of honeybees come from southern Europe. Queen bees of Italian origin are commonly advertised in beekeeping journals.

Until 1621, no *Apis* honeybees existed in North or South America. Then colonists brought hives on their sailing ships, and European varieties of honeybees have thrived ever since in the temperate climate of North America. They are kept in large commercial *apiaries* (a collection of hives) and by many thousands of amateur beekeepers. Honeybees also live in the wild, nesting in hollow trees and other natural shelters, just as their ancestors did long ago in Europe.

The origins of so-called killer bees lie in Africa, where honeybees faced very different conditions from those in Europe. Most of the continent has a tropical climate without a long cold season. Honeybees do not need to store honey for winter survival, nor do they need to nest inside trees for protection against the cold. As a result, African bees build rather small nests that contain less honey than do those of European honeybees.

Many colonies, especially in arid regions, make nests out in the open—on a tree branch or in a rocky crevice. This leaves the nest vulnerable to attack. For millions of years, African bees have contended with predators such as ants, honey badgers, and people. Only the most unapproachable colonies survived. For their own protection, they became easily provoked and highly defensive.

An alarm scent from one disturbed worker bee may trigger defensive action by hundreds or thousands of others. African bees respond more quickly, stay agitated longer, and chase enemies farther than European varieties of honeybees. The sting of an African bee is no more dangerous than that of other honeybees, but several hundred tiny doses of venom from any kind of bee can be fatal. (For details about the health dangers of African bees, see "For Your Safety," page 46.)

The fierce temperament of African bees must always be kept in mind. In 1974, William Lyon, an American entomologist, taught at the University of Nairobi in Kenya. An amateur beekeeper in his home state of Ohio, Lyon had also successfully transferred swarms of wild African honeybees into hives at the university without mishap. One hive remained empty, and he was asked to investigate a colony living inside a wall of a new house in a nearby village. As long as the bees remained, the house couldn't be rented. Lyon and his assistant drove to the village. They donned hats, veils, gloves, and overalls, and they then urged the women and children of the village to stay back at least forty to fifty yards.

Without warning, Lyon's assistant ripped some siding from the house. "That was the mistake!" Lyon wrote later. "Bees came boiling out of their nest literally by the thousands, swarming and stinging everything in sight. . . . The women, children, and livestock were soon reached. Most everyone seemed to be crying and screaming, covering their bodies with blankets. . . .

Wild honeybees in the United States and Canada are European varieties that nest in hollow trees (left). African honeybees may build nests out in the open (right).

The bees entered the huts by the hundreds, stinging old persons who were unaware of what was happening."

Bees crawled under Lyon's veil, stinging him on his ears, nose, cheeks, eyelids, and forehead. He wore low shoes, and was stung about fifty times on his ankles and lower legs. Lyon and his assistant ran to the car and jumped in, accompanied by several hundred bees.

The two of them returned with insecticide and sprayed the nest area and some pigs and goats that were lying on the ground. Bees were still stinging anything that moved an hour and a half after they were disturbed. William Lyon feared that he had earned the hatred of the villagers, but later he learned that matters had ended well. Two goats and a chicken had died from stings, but all of the people had recovered. The bees fled, and so the house could be rented. Furthermore, from within the wall of the house, the villagers recovered two washtubs full of honey.

Because African honeybees do not need large stores of honey for winter, they are free to swarm more frequently than bees from a temperate climate. African bees use more cells for raising their young than for honey storage. This causes a hive population to grow rapidly, setting the stage for swarming.

African bees are also quick to abandon a nest, which is called *absconding*. A fire near a nest, or any other disturbance, may cause the entire colony to flee. They abscond most frequently in the wet season, and also at the end of a long dry season. Because winter cold does not loom ahead, African bees can abandon their combs and set off in search of a better nectar-foraging area. European honeybees rarely abscond, even when living in the tropics. For example, during the rainy season in French Guinea, when few plants bloom, colonies of European honeybees died out rather than abandon their hives.

Despite their tendencies to abscond and to sting, African honeybees are kept in great numbers by African people. In some parts of East Africa, more than half of the population keep honeybees. Beekeepers avoid disturbing their bees in daylight and usually remove honey and beeswax at night, when they suffer fewer stings.

Some South African beekeepers run large commercial apiaries. One beekeeper produces eighty tons of honey each year from fifteen hundred bee colonies. To replace colonies that abscond, the keeper sets out hives along routes commonly traveled by swarming bees. In one year he caught more than seven hundred colonies in this way. To counter the fierce defensive behavior of the bees, up to sixty hives are kept inside specially designed houses in which people can work safely without being stung much. Thus, when people have an understanding of the bees and are able to make or buy the right equipment, they can extract a bounty of honey and beeswax from African bees in certain tropical environments.

When African bees sense that their nest is threatened, thousands of worker bees may fly out to sting the intruder.

2
BIRTH OF A
LEGEND

For more than a century, beekeepers in Africa and in South America imported European honeybees, but these temperate-zone bees did not fare well in much of the tropics. In the 1950s, the Brazilian government tried to find ways to boost national honey production. One step was to support bee-breeding research by geneticist Warwick Kerr at the University of São Paulo.

Kerr knew that African honeybees could be good honey producers, so in 1956, he imported a number of African queens in order to conduct some captive cross-breeding experiments. He also knew of the savage reputation of African bees and of the potential folly in releasing an alien organism into a new environment. This often has bad results, as demonstrated by destruction caused by gypsy moths, introduced to North America; and by European rabbits, introduced to Australia.

Kerr reportedly took special precautions to prevent escape of the queen bees. However, his research had barely begun in 1957, when African queens and their swarms of drones and workers escaped. African honeybees were loose in Brazil.

They soon demonstrated their superiority to temperate-zone bees in a tropical environment. European races never had established much of a feral population in Latin America, as they commonly do in cooler climates. (Domesticated animals gone wild and their descendants are called *feral*.) The African queens and their swarms readily nested in the wild. Reproducing quickly and swarming frequently, African bees began to spread in all directions.

The African bees overwhelmed European bees kept in apiaries. In some areas, they robbed hives of honey or took over hives, killing the less aggressive occupants. African drones mated with European queens, and the following generations retained the aggressiveness of their fathers. Their savage defensiveness surprised and alarmed Brazilians. In Brazil, as in other Latin American countries, most beehives were kept near homes and roads, close to where people live and travel. People were accustomed to the presence of docile European honey-

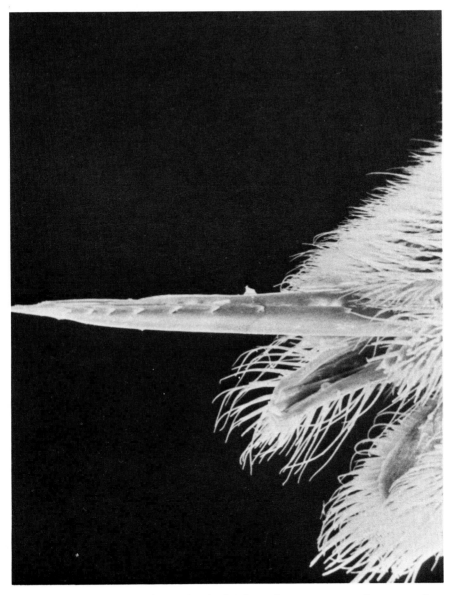

The stinger and venom of an individual African bee are no more dangerous than those of other varieties of honeybees, but a person who accidentally disturbs African bees may be stung hundreds of times.

bees. Suddenly they found that a slight disturbance sparked stinging attacks by hundreds of bees.

A few horrifying incidents, given wide publicity, helped create the legend of the killer bees. One man was found dead with a thousand stings on his head; he had shot himself to end his agony. Another man, on horseback, collided with a swarm of African bees. The horse threw him to the ground, breaking the man's leg, and then ran off with the bees in pursuit. Three days later the horse died from the countless stings it had received.

Each year brings new incidents that show how deadly African bees can be. In July 1986, a 24-year-old graduate student at the University of Miami accidentally disturbed a bee nest in Costa Rica. He was on an afternoon field trip to a cave with some other students, and was exploring alone among rocks above the cave entrance. His companions heard him shout and saw him thrashing his arms around his head, surrounded by a cloud of bees. He disappeared behind a boulder and stopped calling after a few minutes.

People who tried to rescue him were driven back by the stinging bees. Two were hospitalized. After dark the student was found dead. He had become wedged in a crevice, could not flee, and had been stung eight thousand times.

Another terrible incident occurred in early 1989. In Panama, three men fishing from a boat on a lake came close to an island where bees nested in a hollow stump. The bees defended their nest and began stinging the men, who dived overboard. The bees continued to sting the swimming men, one of whom died by drowning.

As these cases show, healthy adults can become victims of African bees when circumstances keep them from escaping. Most victims are older men, people who are physically handicapped, or children under eight years of age. Since the bees defend their colony so swiftly, people who are unable to take cover or flee can be stung several hundred times in a few minutes. Massive stinging seems to cause heart or kidney failure, but there are other causes of death from multiple bee stings, and more knowledge is needed in order to develop effective medical treatment.

Alarming though such incidents are, they give a false impression of African bees. First, they sting only to defend their hive or swarm. Second, stinging incidents involving large numbers of bees are not common. They kill many fewer people than sensational stories in newspapers, magazines, and other media would have you believe.

DON'T ATTACK THE AFRICANIZED BEES warns a poster in Panama. Once people learn to avoid the bees, stinging incidents decrease.

Accurate data on bee-sting deaths in Latin America are difficult to obtain. A reasonable estimate indicates that between 700 and 1,000 people died between 1957 and 1985. This is not a large number, considering the time period, geographic area, and size of the human population. In fact, it is less than 40 fatalities a year. European honeybees in the United States kill about that many people annually. Most victims are allergic to bee venom and may die from just one sting. As such, the comparatively docile European honeybees might be as deserving of the term *killer bee* as the African honeybee.

Although deaths caused by African bees are fewer than most people imagine, the bees send many people to doctors or hospitals for treatment. There may be 100 to 200 such cases for each fatality.

Stinging incidents follow patterns. Most occur during the honeybee swarming season. Also, most fatalities occur during the first four years after African bees invade a region. After that period, most people learn to avoid encounters with the bees, and the number of deaths from stings declines. Another factor that affects deaths caused by bees is the density of the human and bee populations. Wherever both people and African bees are abundant, a certain number of stinging incidents is inevitable, and some people die.

Even though their killer reputation has been exaggerated, African bees have driven thousands of Latin American beekeepers out of business. As the bees spread outward from southeastern Brazil, they took over all existing colonies of European honeybees. Their tendency to sting and abscond readily discouraged most beekeepers.

In Brazil, more than half of all beekeepers abandoned or destroyed their apiaries. The same occurred in other nations as African honeybees moved southwest into Paraguay and Argentina, west into Bolivia and Peru, and north into Surinam, Venezuela, Colombia, and beyond. Honey production fell. Venezuela, for example, had a harvest of 578 tons of honey in 1975. African bees reached Venezuela in 1977, and by 1981, the honey harvest had fallen to 100 tons.

In 1984, Dr. Orley "Chip" Taylor, entomologist at the University of Kansas and an authority on African bees, reported in the *American Bee Journal* that "Beekeeping still appears to be severely depressed in Paraguay, Uruguay, Bolivia, Surinam, Guyana, Venezuela, and is presently declining in Peru, Ecuador, Colombia, and Trinidad. Declines in production should also soon be evident in Panama and Costa Rica."

His prediction proved to be correct. Panama was a honey-exporting nation and had about 20,000 colonies of managed European honeybees in 1982, when African bees invaded. By the late 1980s, many beekeepers had quit. Only 8,000 colonies were managed, and Panama had to import honey to meet its needs.

From southern Brazil, however, came reports of increasing honey production. After a difficult period of adjustment, commercial beekeepers had a better understanding of African bees and were learning to manage them better.

Respecting the famed defensiveness of the bees, keepers moved hives more than six hundred feet from homes and livestock. (Hives could be closer if bushes and trees screened the bees from potential disturbance.) Individual hives were set farther apart than before, and beekeepers learned to move quietly and slowly near their bees. Veils, bee suits, and other protective wear proved to be vital, though uncomfortably hot in the tropics.

If a colony was especially aggressive, beekeepers removed its queen, replacing it with the daughter of a queen of a less defensive colony. Such colonies became less aggressive and usually were also good honey producers. To keep African bees from absconding, keepers fed colonies when flower nectar was scarce and also made sure there was plenty of hive space. (A sense of becoming crowded, or running out of space, stimulates swarming behavior in honeybees.)

Brazilian beekeepers began to view African bees as an asset instead of a problem. In one area, European bees in an apiary produced just 20 pounds of honey in a month and a half, whereas African bees in the same apiary produced 77 pounds in that time. Brazilian beekeepers also discovered that honey could be produced in northeastern Brazil, a region where European honeybees had done poorly. The climate of northeastern Brazil is like that of the semiarid regions of Africa, where African bees thrive. The existence of feral colonies of African bees also provided some peasants with a new kind of livelihood as hunters of wild honey.

The glowing reports from Brazil seemed to contradict everything people had heard about African bees. Would honey production also rebound in other Latin American nations? In 1984, Dr. Orley Taylor offered his opinion: "In my view the recovery of the industry in southern Brazil is the exception and not the rule."

He warned that recovery in other countries would come only from training of beekeepers and changes in their attitudes. He also questioned whether African bees are really superior to European bees throughout the tropics. In the dry habitat of western Venezuela, European bees used to produce 100 to 200 pounds of honey per hive in a year. As they foraged near their apiaries, these bees had no competition from feral honeybees.

Now there is a large feral population of African bees that competes for nectar with bees from apiaries. Whether beekeepers have European or African bees in their hives, they seldom get more than 65 pounds of honey a year. The beekeepers are trying to survive on a third of the honey they once harvested and are faced with rising costs of managing the African bees. "It is worth remembering," wrote Orley Taylor, "that the so-called 'superior' honey production by African bees has put many beekeepers out of business."

Generally, in areas where flowering plants are scarce, African bees are more successful than European bees at honey making. European bees are best where foraging conditions are good, as they are in most of the United States.

African bees forage for food while swarming to obtain the energy to fly many miles before settling into a new nest.

3

SWARMING NORTHWARD

African honeybees reached the United States on their own in 1990. However, they had been brought in earlier, by accident, traveling inside pipes or other equipment transported by ship. On two occasions, swarms of African bees were discovered aboard the luxury liner *Queen Elizabeth II* as she passed through the Panama Canal. Dozens of other swarms have also been found and destroyed on ships passing through the canal.

In the United States, the most notable outbreak of African bees occurred in 1985, in central California. A massive search-and-destroy operation in an area measuring 400 square miles located twelve colonies of African bees. One problem that added to the cost of this effort was simply distinguishing these bees from their European relatives.

African bees look like other honeybees. They are a bit smaller, weigh a bit less, and have shorter tongues and forewings. The six-sided cells they build in their nests are also measurably smaller than those of European honeybees. But no single physical characteristic sets African bees apart from other honeybees. So far the most reliable identification method requires twenty-five different body measurements. Feeding these data into a computer enables entomologists to identify correctly African bees about 95 percent of the time.

In scientific research and in beekeeping, it is often important to identify killer bees while they are still alive. People who are familiar with both varieties of honeybees can identify live African bees by their behavior. They are more nervous than European bees within their hives, as well as at their entrances. In flight, African honeybees move more rapidly and in a more noticeable zigzag motion than European bees.

In 1989, researchers at the Oak Ridge National Laboratory developed a device that identifies African bees by the sound their wings make. They discovered that African bees move their wings at a higher frequency than European bees. African bees have a noticeably different buzz, which can be detected when a live bee is placed inside a small plastic cylinder attached to a microphone. The first version of this "Buzz-Buster" de-

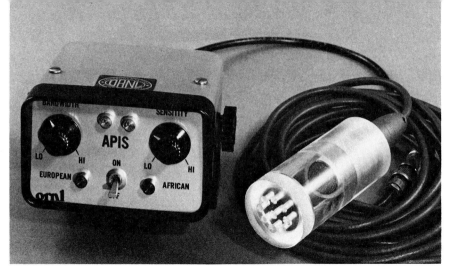

The "Buzz-Buster" may help field-workers identify African bees—which beat their wings about fifty more times a second than European bees—with some accuracy. It measures the sound frequency made by the wings of live bees put in the plastic cylinder at right.

vice flashed a green light for the sound of European honeybees, a red light for African bees. The newest model emits a warning sound when an African bee is identified.

Beginning in the 1970s, Dr. Orley Taylor traveled widely in Latin America, both into areas where African bees had taken over and places they had not invaded. One of his research goals was to chart the movements of the bees and to predict how fast and far they would spread.

Dr. Taylor found that African honeybees spread most rapidly in dry habitats, especially coastal savannas (areas of grassland, scattered trees, and small patches of forest). This habitat is similar to that in East Africa, where African honeybees thrive. The bees advanced more slowly through the interior rain forest.

In their first few years in Brazil, the range of African

Dr. Orley "Chip" Taylor began studying African bees in 1974.

bees expanded outward about fifty miles a year. By 1963, large numbers of colonies had been established, and the bees' range began to increase dramatically through dry regions. Now the bees advanced at a pace of three hundred miles a year.

This astonished people who knew only European bees. According to the most detailed study of European swarms, bees scouting for a new nest site fly up to 2.7 miles, but their swarms usually settle into a nest within a mile of their former home. No one knows how far, on the average, swarms of African bees travel before re-nesting. (Swarming bees *do* pause to rest and sometimes to feed.) Their African ancestors reportedly have flown nearly a hundred miles. In South America, African bees have established populations on islands that are separated from the mainland by 14 miles of open ocean. A Brazilian beekeeper claimed that he followed, by car and bicycle, a swarm of bees a distance of 175 miles. Thus, with each colony able to produce a new swarm just fifty days after nesting, African bees clearly are able to occupy new territory at a dizzying pace.

Based on his findings in Latin America, Orley Taylor in 1975 assumed that African honeybees would move northward at a rate of two to three hundred miles each year. The bees have stayed on schedule.

Taylor also tried to determine how far north in the northern hemisphere these tropical insects could survive. Some clues came from the distribution of the African honeybee on its native continent and from the range of African bees in Argentina. Both Africa and

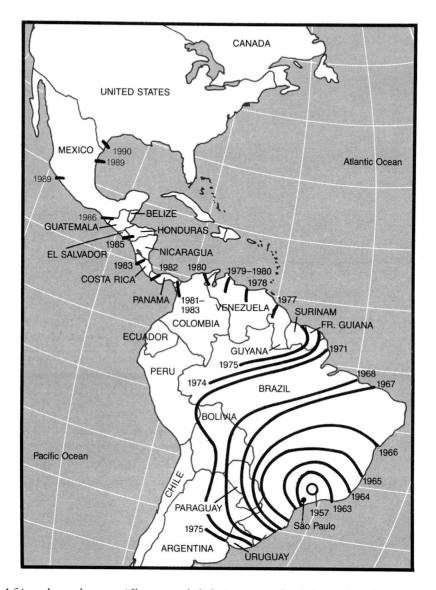

African honeybees rapidly expanded their range after being released in Brazil in 1957. They reached southern Mexico in 1986 and Texas in 1990. They probably will spread eastward along the Gulf Coast at a pace of about two hundred miles a year.

26

Argentina are in the southern hemisphere, so the farther south the bees range, the cooler the climate.

In Argentina, the success of the bees declined as they spread into cooler climates. In a zone that includes Argentina's capital, Buenos Aires, African bees established colonies in the summer but failed to survive most winters.

North of that zone the bees lived year-round. A key difference between the two areas seemed to be the mean (average) high temperature of the coldest month, which in Argentina is July. African bees died in places where the mean maximum temperature in July was below 60 degrees Fahrenheit, or 16 degrees Celsius. They survived if the mean maximum was 60 degrees F or above.

Orley Taylor and his colleague at the University of Kansas, Marla Spivak, decided that the 60 degree F line in January—the coldest month in the United States— would be the best predictor of the northern limit of African bees. The line roughly marks the regions where winter (the period from first to last frost) is four months or more in duration.

The map on page 28 shows the probable range of African bees in the United States. It extends up to Santa Cruz, California, on the West Coast and near Fayetteville, North Carolina, on the East. The bees will find a favorable climate in parts of twelve states. Nearly all of Florida, for example, has a mean high temperature in January of 66 degrees F or 19 degrees C. In similar climates elsewhere, African bees have been highly successful, making up all captive and feral colonies. Southern Florida, with its warm climate and limestone rock riddled with nest holes, is an excellent African bee habitat. Large populations of African bees will also occupy southern Louisiana and southern Texas. African bees will also replace European honeybees in the southern parts of Georgia, Mississippi, Arizona, and California.

Orley Taylor believes that in somewhat colder regions of the United States, African bees and European bees will probably coexist, as they do in parts of Argentina. In still colder areas, where the mean high temperature in January is below 60 degrees F, African bees still may appear in the summer as they swarm northward or are spread accidentally by people. Mild winters will enable them to survive for a while beyond their usual overwintering zone. Harsh winters will wipe out these northern outposts.

Some other entomologists believe that the range of African bees will reach much farther north, perhaps into Canada. Entomologist Albert Dietz of the University of

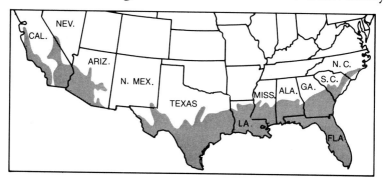

African bees probably will live year-round in the region shown in gray. Farther north of that area, they probably will survive in summertime and during years having mild winters.

Georgia forecast that African bees could live in such places as northern California and the Boston, Massachusetts, area. He based his conclusions on observations of bee colonies set out in winter in Argentina and colonies kept in a refrigeration chamber. He found that African and European honeybees survived equally well.

However, the "African" bees that Dietz tested were collected in an area of Argentina where both African and European bees coexist. The bees crossbreed, and many apiary colonies have characteristics of both varieties. According to Orley Taylor, there is no evidence that true African bees can survive winters of five months or longer in the central and northern United States. If they could, wild African bees would now live in the Buenos Aires province of Argentina. They do not.

With African bees reaching Texas in 1990, people wonder how soon they will occupy the rest of their potential range. This depends on several factors, including possible human efforts to block or slow the bees. The African bees that first entered Texas were descendants of bees that swarmed along Mexico's eastern coast. As the map on page 26 shows, bees moving along Mexico's western coast must travel much farther before reaching California. The arid climate along that coast has also slowed the bees. African bees may reach southern Arizona in 1993 and southern California in 1994 or 1995.

Swarming eastward from Texas, African bees could colonize territory as far as North Carolina by about 1998, if people do nothing to stop them.

In the Bee Regulated Zone and farther north in Mexico, baited hives were set out to attract swarms of African bees, which were then killed.

4

ADVANCING THROUGH MEXICO, AND STILL AFRICAN

Mexico was the last place where African bees could be stopped from reaching the United States. For decades, the goal of somehow blocking the northward march of the bees was wished for by many people and actively studied by a few. Had a method of stopping African bees been ready, Panama, the narrowest of Central American countries, would have been the place to implement it. The bees swept through Panama during 1982–1983.

They reached southern Mexico late in 1986. And in 1987, Mexico and the United States agreed to make a belated effort in Mexico that some believed would halt the spread of African bees. Many scientists were skeptical about the Bee Regulated Zone (BRZ), as it was called. At best, they said, the program was only a delaying tactic.

The BRZ was established at Mexico's narrowest part, the Isthmus of Tehuantepec. Scientists from the U.S. Department of Agriculture and their Mexican allies planned several tactics to halt African bees. Bounties were offered to citizens who reported swarms or feral colonies. Thirty thousand baited hives were spread throughout the zone. They were baited with chemical substances called *pheromones,* which attracted swarms of African bees that were then killed.

Plans called for "flooding" the BRZ with drones of the European variety that would mate with African queen bees that entered the BRZ, but this was not carried out.

African bees entered the BRZ in the spring or early summer of 1988. Any illusions about actually stopping their progress were soon lost. By October 1988, swarms of African bees had crossed most of the hundred-mile-wide BRZ, reaching its northern edge and continuing northward. African bees continued to enter the BRZ from the south. As many as four hundred swarms were caught and killed during some weeks in 1989. But there was no evidence that the BRZ had slowed African bees appreciably.

Many Mexican beekeepers within the BRZ gave the program halfhearted support. Entomologists had hoped that African bees would encounter 80,000 managed colonies of European bees in the BRZ, but the number dwindled to near 20,000. Beekeepers were offered incentives to stay but preferred moving their hives, as usual, closer to rich sources of flower nectar in other areas. Some beekeepers refused to kill bee colonies that had been invaded by African queens.

According to the BRZ plan, an abundance of European bee colonies would help "dilute" the genetic characteristics of wild African bees. In theory, crossbreeding would produce feral African bees that would behave more like European bees. Many bee researchers were skeptical about this idea. In 1988, entomologist Roger Morse of Cornell University said, "To talk of genetic dilution is ridiculous. It hasn't happened in the thirty-one years since the bees arrived in Brazil."

Orley Taylor agreed. He said, "These bees are African. They are not diluted. They are maintaining their genetic integrity. . . . They are going to reach us essentially unchanged."

He is among a growing number of scientists who call the bees *African*, not Africanized. Bees that are hybrids of European and African parents can be called Africanized, but they do not seem to survive as well in the wild as true African bees. It is the African queens that thrive, swarm, colonize new territory, and pass their characteristics on to new generations of honeybees. Research reported in 1989 by Taylor, Glenn Hall of the University of Florida, and others showed that African bees had not changed genetically through 150 generations and over a span of 30 years as they traveled more than 5,000 miles from Brazil to Mexico.

Mexico is a major honey producer. Its beekeepers collect more than 146 million pounds of honey annually from more than 2.5 million hives. Although honeybee management is primitive in some areas, especially the Yucatán Peninsula, many Mexican beekeepers use modern techniques and equipment with their European bees. Mexico's central highlands is home to some of the world's largest beekeeping operations.

Mexico's beekeepers face troubled times, however. In 1988, Hurricane Gilbert destroyed up to 80 percent of the European honeybee colonies in parts of the Yucatán Peninsula. And most amateur beekeepers and poorly trained commercial beekeepers will have difficulty adapting to African bees.

One vital factor in managing hives of African bees is the ability to replace their queens with queens of docile European varieties. However, imported queens are too costly for most Mexican beekeepers. Mexico needs to produce two million of its own European queens annually and also teach inexperienced beekeepers how to re-queen their colonies. Mexican beekeepers also need bee suits, veils, and large smoke-producing devices (smoke calms honeybees and African bees usually require heavy doses). The cost of this gear also may be beyond the means of many Mexican beekeepers.

Another source of trouble lies in the intense nature of beekeeping in Mexico. In some regions apiaries occupy every available site. Many are located close to people

Although African honeybees can be managed, the extra effort and cost of protective clothing and smoke-producing devices may drive many beekeepers out of business.

Apiaries of African honeybees cannot be close to homes or livestock. More space between individual hives helps keep one colony from alarming others.

and livestock, and there will be no place to relocate them away from potential disturbance when African bees take over.

Some of Mexico's commercial beekeepers moved their colonies to higher, cooler elevations to delay trouble with African bees. Several years will pass before African bees occupy all suitable habitats in Mexico. In some areas, European bees may hold their own against the invaders. African bees are tropical insects and may reach their climatic limits in the coldest regions of Mexico.

In 1990, African bees began to meet large populations of European bees in Texas. Later they will also encounter many feral and managed European honeybee colonies farther along the Gulf Coast. This will be a real test of the mating success of African bees. In somewhat colder regions, the two varieties of honeybees probably will be about equal in their ability to survive. In these "hybrid zones," neither variety will dominate. Wherever African bees achieve a greater population density, they will soon overwhelm their European rivals.

The outcome in the United States is still in doubt and may not be clear for a decade. There is no doubt, however, that there will be trouble for people while the bees work it out.

In warm climates, African bees have a mating advantage over other honeybee varieties. By learning more about bee reproduction, entomologists may yet find a way to "tame" African honeybees.

5

IMPACT IN THE UNITED STATES

The advancing front of African bees is hard to detect.
Low numbers of colonies are widely scattered. With the
experience of Latin American countries as a guide, Texas
can expect African bees to reach peak numbers between
1992 and 1995—two to five years after the bees first
cross the border from Mexico.

In the Southwest, African bees are likely to be most
numerous and troublesome in urban areas, according
to John G. Thomas, extension entomologist at Texas
A&M University. In cities and suburbs, the bees will
find an abundance of nest sites and flowering plants

that do not exist on the open range and on cropland.

As African honeybees invade parts of the southern United States, many people will focus on their reputation as "killer bees." The bees' actual threat to public health is real but limited. Some people will die. For each fatality there will also be numerous incidents of multiple stings that require medical treatment. (For advice on avoiding these hazards, see "For Your Safety," following this chapter.) African bees will also take a toll on livestock, pets, and wild animals.

The defensive stinging of African bees is serious, but this problem is dwarfed by other troubles the bees may bring. Beekeepers are worried about changes in attitude toward honeybees and their business. Darrell Lister, former president of the beekeeper's association in Houston, Texas, said in 1988, "I'm afraid we are going to have a panic that will devastate the bee industry. Everyone will be out with a spray can, and the only good bee will be a dead bee."

Beekeepers are concerned that county and community governments will ban the keeping of honeybees, or impose other conditions that will put them out of business. They fear lawsuits over stinging incidents, and high insurance costs. Beekeepers as far north as New Jersey have expressed concern that stinging incidents in the South will generate opposition to their business or hobby.

An estimated 200,000 people in the United States keep honeybees as a hobby or small business. Within the range of African bees, many hobbyists will abandon their hives because of the increased cost and difficulty of dealing with African bees. For this reason, and as a result of African bees replacing European bees as foragers in some areas, honey production in the United States will drop.

Even more serious will be the effect of African bees on firms that raise queen bees and "packages" of bees for starting colonies. More than 90 percent of the package- and queen-rearing business in the United States occurs within the zone where African bees are likely to survive in all seasons. Many beekeepers replace queen bees annually to ensure high honey yields from their colonies. Each spring young queens are shipped to thousands of beekeepers all over the United States and Canada. These beekeepers will not want queens that have mated with African drones. So the people who raise queens and bee packages must somehow keep African drones from mating with their European queens. Failing that, they will have to relocate their businesses to northern sites beyond the reach of African bees.

The African bee invasion will strike a queen- and package-rearing business that was already in trouble. In the late 1980s, two species of tiny Asian mites that weaken and kill European honeybees somehow reached Florida. By the end of 1989, the varroa mite had spread to bee colonies of eighteen states. In the winter of 1988–1989, well over 200,000 colonies died from infestations of tracheal mites. Entomologists have found some honeybees that are resistant to mites and hope to develop stocks of mite-resistant queens for beekeepers. In the meantime, beekeepers are wary of ordering bees that might be infested with mites, so queen- and package-rearing companies are losing business. Under economic stress, the honeybee industry may not be able to respond well to the African bee challenge.

The African bees' greatest threat, however, is not to health or to the queen- and package-rearing business but to flower pollination that is provided by European honeybees. The value of European bees to United States agriculture has been estimated at $20 billion. Honeybees account for about 80 percent of all insect pollination of agricultural crops in the United States.

In California alone, honeybee pollination of about fifty crops is valued at $4 billion a year. Bee pollination is vital to ninety vegetable, fruit, seed, and nut crops, including cucumbers, muskmelons, oranges, nectarines, peaches, apples, alfalfa, and almonds. Such foods as cucumbers and apples require bees for pollination; other foods, including berries and cherries, develop in greater abundance and are of better quality when pollinated by bees.

Some of this pollination is done for free by bees from feral colonies or from hives kept by hobbyists. A great deal of agricultural pollination is done by bees, provided by commercial bee-rearing firms that transport honeybees from one flowering crop to the next. For example, bees from the South are trucked to pollinate some of New York's apple trees. Some Wisconsin bees are taken to Florida in winter to pollinate crops of bell peppers and watermelons. Hives from other states are trucked

In the United States, the value of honeybee flower pollination is estimated at $20 billion a year. Many thousands of hives are trucked from place to place as different food crops come into flower.

into California's almond orchards when the trees begin to flower.

This pollination service will be disrupted by the presence of African bees in the Sunbelt. One commercial beekeeper in California predicted a catastrophe, saying, "We beekeepers could gear up to handle them, but the irrigators, harvesters, and tractor drivers—the people who have to work in the fields—would have an awful time."

Most people in the United States will never encounter African bees, but everyone may be stung by a scarcity of certain foods, as well as higher prices for some bee-pollinated agricultural products.

Considering the potential harm that can be caused by African bees, many bee researchers have been appalled at the lack of funds provided for research. According to Orley Taylor, between $3 and $5 million was spent between 1971 and 1988. If the United States had spent that much annually during the 1980s, it would be better prepared for the African bees.

Invasion by African bees was predicted many years ago. Now the bees are here, and the U.S. Department of Agriculture and state agencies face the threat with no single, easy, proven method of identifying African bees with complete accuracy. They have no methods of proven effectiveness for locating, attacking, and killing feral colonies or swarms of African bees. State governments, beginning with Texas, now have no choice but to spend millions of dollars in an attempt to control

African bees, step up the inspection and regulation of the beekeeping business, and teach citizens how to avoid trouble with the bees.

Even though money for research has failed to match the serious need, entomologists have learned much in the past few years. The African honeybee has forced them to ask some fundamental and important questions about bee biology and genetics.

The answers to those questions will give scientists a better understanding of bee behavior and reproduction. Entomologists may yet discover a way to give European honeybees a mating advantage over African bees. If that occurs, the future of beekeeping, of honey production, and of many agricultural crops in the United States will look brighter.

FOR YOUR SAFETY

Although so-called killer bees are not a major health hazard, some commonsense precautions should be taken if you live or visit within their range. Remember, the bees do not seek victims but do defend their nests and swarms aggressively. People can coexist with the bees without giving up outdoor activities by learning about the bees' behavior and being alert to their presence.

- The main danger is an accidental encounter with a wild colony of African bees. However, it is also wise to keep several hundred feet away from hives in managed apiaries and to avoid disturbing the bees in any way.
- Be alert for colonies of African bees. They may nest in stone walls or underground holes, and even in such places as birdhouses, discarded tires, and empty flowerpots.
- Also watch out for flying or resting swarms of African bees. In the United States their peak swarming season will be in the summer months.

- If African bees start to sting, flee as quickly as you can. (If possible, release penned animals so they can escape.) Seek shelter in a building, car, or other structure. If there is no shelter available, run behind shrubs, trees, a fence, or other obstacles that block the bees' line of vision.
- Don't attempt to return and kill the bees yourself. Report the nest or swarm to the police or other authorities, which will notify the agency in charge of African bee control.
- For most people a few bee stings cause nothing more harmful than some painful swelling. However, anyone who has been stung and who feels dizzy, has difficulty breathing, or who has been stung fifty times or more should be treated by a doctor as soon as possible.

GLOSSARY

abscond—to leave quickly and secretly. Swarms of African honeybees abscond frequently, a characteristic that makes them more difficult to manage than European varieties of honeybees.

Africanized bees—hybrids that have characteristics of both African and European varieties of honeybees. Most entomologists now apply this term only to bees from areas where African and European bees coexist, at the limits of the range of African bees. Elsewhere in the New World, African bees are basically the same variety that was released in Brazil in 1957.

allergy—an especially sensitive or extreme reaction to an environmental factor or substance in amounts that do not affect most people. People who are allergic to bee venom can die from a single sting.

apiary—a place where honeybee colonies are kept in a collection of hives and raised for their honey.

crossbreeding—mating individuals of different varieties, producing offspring (hybrids) that may have desirable characteristics of both parents.

drone—the male honeybee, which does not work and lacks a sting. Drones live from late spring to the end of the summer. Their role is to mate with a queen, and their large eyes are an adaptation for seeing a queen bee on her mating flight. Drones die soon after mating.

entomology—the scientific study of insects.

evolution—the process by which the characteristics of a population or entire species of organisms gradually change over a period of time.

feral—existing in the wild after having been domesticated. Tame animals gone wild, and their descendants, are called *feral*.

genetics—the study of the heredity of living things, or how parents pass characteristics on to their offspring.

hybrid—the offspring produced by breeding plants or animals of different varieties, such as two varieties of honeybees.

hybridization—the process of producing hybrids.

pheromone—a chemical message produced by an animal, transmitted as an odor, that induces behavioral or other changes in other animals of the same kind. An alarm pheromone, for example, induces worker bees to sting, and a pheromone released by a queen bee attracts drones to mate with her.

pollen—the male sex cells of flowering plants.

pollination—the process of conveying or transferring pollen from an anther to a stigma of a flower. When male sex cells (pollen grains) reach female sex cells, fertilization occurs. The fertilized eggs then develop into seeds. In their quest for food, honeybees and other insects accidentally spread pollen around and play a vital role in pollination.

queen—the sexually fertile female that is the heart of a colony of social bees, including honeybees. A queen honeybee may live for several years, during which she can lay a million eggs. The fertilized eggs she lays develop into worker bees or queens (one of which will eventually replace her); unfertilized eggs develop into drones.

species—a population or many populations of an organism that have characteristics in common, which make them different from individuals of other populations. The members of a species crossbreed with each other but not with members of other species. Thus, different populations of honeybees crossbreed, but honeybees cannot crossbreed with other bee species.

swarm—a group of honeybees, with its queen, emigrating to a new nest site. Usually at least half of a colony's workers and drones accompany a queen. Before swarming, the bees fill themselves with honey, for they usually go without food until scout bees locate a new home. However, African bees sometimes forage for food while swarming; this enables their swarms to travel great distances.

worker—the infertile female bee that does virtually all the work in a honeybee colony. Workers are the builders, cleaners, nurses, honey makers, and defenders of their colony.

FURTHER READING

Anonymous. *Final Report: Committee on the African Honeybee.* Washington, D.C.: National Academy of Sciences, 1972.

Booth, William. "USDA Fights to Repeal African Bees' Invasion." *Science,* October 21, 1988, pp. 368–369.

Bradbear, Nocola, and David DeJong. *The Management of Africanized Honeybees.* Leaflet #2, International Bee Research Association.

Breed, M. D., and A. J. Moore. "The Guard Bee as a Component of the Defensive Response." In *Africanized Bees and Bee Mites.* New York: Wiley, 1988, pp. 105–109.

Collins, Anita, et al. "Colony Defense by Africanized and European Honey Bees." *Science,* October 1, 1982, pp. 72–74.

Fletcher, David, and Michael Breed, editors. *The "African" Honey Bee.* Boulder, Colorado: Westview Press, 1987.

Fore, Troy. "African or Africanized—The Bees Are Still Coming." *The Speedy Bee,* June 1989, pp. 1, 7, 10.

Garelik, Glenn. "The Killers." *Discover,* October 1985, pp. 108–115.

Gore, Rick. "Those Fiery Brazilian Bees." *National Geographic,* April 1976, pp. 491–501.

Laidlaw, H. H., Jr. "Thoughts on Countering the Africanized-Bee Threat." In *Africanized Bees and Bee Mites.* New York: Wiley, 1988, pp. 209–213.

Longgood, William. *The Queen Must Die, and Other Affairs of Bees and Men.* New York: W. W. Norton & Company, 1985.

Lyon, William F. "My Experience with the African Honeybee." *Gleanings in Bee Culture,* November 1974, pp. 335–336.

Moffett, J. O., and D. L. Maki. "Venezuela and the Africanized Bee." *American Bee Journal,* Vol. 128, no. 12 (1988), pp. 827–830.

Morse, Roger. *The Complete Guide to Beekeeping.* New York: E. P. Dutton, 1974.

Needham, Glen, et al., editors. *Africanized Honey Bees and Bee Mites.* New York: Wiley, 1988.

Page, Robert. "Neotropical African Bees." *Nature,* May 18, 1989, pp. 181–182.

Rinderer, T., et al. "Nectar-Foraging Characteristics of Africanized and European Honeybees in the Neotropics." *Journal of Apicultural Research,* Vol. 23, no. 2 (1984), pp. 70–79.

Seeley, T. D. "What We Do and Do Not Know about Nest-Site Preferences of African Honey Bees." In *Africanized Bees and Bee Mites.* New York: Wiley, 1988, pp. 87–90.

Taylor, Orley. "African Bees: Potential Impact in the United States." *Bulletin of the Entomological Society of America,* Winter 1985, pp. 15–24.

Taylor, Orley. "Ecology and Economic Impact on African and Africanized Honey Bees." In *Africanized Honey Bees and Bee Mites.* New York: Wiley, 1988, pp. 29–41.

Taylor, Orley. "Health Problems Associated with African Bees." *Annals of Internal Medicine,* February 1986, pp. 267–268.

Taylor, Orley. "The Past and Possible Future Spread of Africanized Honeybees in the Americas." *Bee World,* Vol. 58, no. 1 (1977), pp. 19–30.

Taylor, Orley, et al. "Genetic Differences Between European and African Bees in Mexico." *American Bee Journal,* December 1988, p. 809 (summary of paper given at 1988 American Bee Research Conference).

Taylor, Orley, et al. "Rate of Spread and Relative Abundance of African Honey Bees in Mexico." *American Bee Journal,* December 1988, pp. 809–810 (summary of paper given at 1988 American Bee Research Conference).

Taylor, Orley, and Marla Spivak. "Climatic Limits of Tropical African Honeybees in the Americas." *Bee World,* Vol. 65, no. 1 (1984), pp. 38–47.

Winston, Mark. "The Potential Impact of the Africanized Honey Bee on Apiculture in Mexico and Central America." *American Bee Journal,* August 1979, pp. 584–586, and September 1979, pp. 642–645.

Winston, Mark, et al. "Absconding Behavior of the Af-

INDEX